A *Sword* in **Both** *Hands*

POEMS RESPONDING TO RUSSIA'S WAR ON UKRAINE

Dick Westheimer

A Sword in Both Hands © Dick Westheimer, 2022
Author Photo © Paul Tinkerhess
Cover Art: Olga Morozova

ISBN: 979-8-9873058-0-5

Sheila-Na-Gig Editions
Russell, KY
Hayley Mitchell Haugen, Editor
www.sheilanagigblog.com

Acknowledgments

With thanks to the editors of the following journals in which these poems first appeared:

Comstock Review: "_____"
The New Verse News: "In the Days Before I Die, I Recall the Last Time I Was Here"
Verse Virtual: "A Ukrainian Woman Confronts a Russian Soldier in Henechesk," "Bodies Responding to Contingent Times"

Many thanks to the journalists who continue to risk their lives to tell the story of Russia's war on Ukraine, members of Poets Muddle Through, my weekly poetics group, who continue to enliven and enrich my reading and writing of poetry—and to my wife, Debbie, generous and incisive first reader of the poems in this collection

To the people of Ukraine
and refugees and truth-tellers everywhere

Table of Contents

Holodomor

All fish disappeared from the river that year
all the songbirds snared from their nests
children scraped the dried fat from the joints
of starved cattle and picked rotted apple cores
from ditches to share with their sisters.

The good died first. The generous died first.
Those who did not eat corpses died first.
Prostitutes survived their johns. The regime
posted fliers noting that eating one's children
was a barbarous act. They said nothing
about eating others'. Beneath the trees,
infants' limbs and wind-blown sticks mixed.

In Paris, the peasants ate cake and my father
summered with his parents. In Berlin,
the Reichstag burned. King Kong lay
dead in the streets of New York
and the Holodomor hid from no one
who paid attention which is the same as
no one except for the *homo horribilis*
stalking the streets of Kyiv and us
thinking it can't happen here.

Near Dawn, Before the War

If civilization has an opposite, it is war.
—Ursula K. Le Guin

In the snow a million miles away,
soldiers shiver in the bellies of tanks
deployed across the border wire
from others huddled in trenches.

Some wear fingerless gloves
and deal cards from a deck stripped
of its lower ranks, 2s and 3s, 4s and 5s,
cast aside for some other gambit.

They play *Durak,* a game as old as Catherine the Great,
lay down cards until only one player,
the fool, is left with any in hand. On both sides
of the wire, cards are shuffled again

are dealt again—and once again
the court cards always win
and the little pips are discarded,
every game the same.

Nearby, snow falls on night-quiet streets.
In one home, someone pulls a loaf of bread from the oven.
In another, an old woman scrubs pots and pans,
her hands pruny and warmed by the dish water.

In a city, not far away,
young clubbers stumble home at first light.
A horn honks. A trash collector idles his truck
and drags a metal bin across the pavement.

A television flickers to life, illuminates a frost-rimmed window
on the twelfth floor of a walk-up in a place named for a saint.
A man unlocks his bicycle. Its chain ticks against the gears
as he pedals down the street.

Another man lights his pipe and reads the morning paper.
A woman steals the last moments of dark to pull
her lover across her night-warm body—one more time—
before she dispatches to the border.

A baby squalls for her mother's milk.
Another cries to have his diaper changed.
In a nearby church, a black-hatted priest
intones Matins: *O Lord, save Thy people.*

Back at the wire, on one side, the men huddled
in the tank play one more hand. In the trench
across the way, a woman collects her buddies' cards,
quietly pockets the suicide king and wonders—

is she more queen or jack or pip?
She pulls out a creased photo of her baby, kisses
it and tucks it in her boot. Dawn tinges the horizon.
She shoulders her pack, checks her rifle
     and heads out on patrol one more time.

A Ukrainian Woman Confronts a Russian Soldier in Henechesk
—After Jericho Brown *Duplex*

Take these seeds and put them in your pocket so at least sunflowers will grow when you lie down to die.
    —An unidentified Ukrainian woman

What seeds will you carry in your pockets when you lie
down among the worms and fungi when you die?

    Above ground we the living won't comply
    with those who come here just to watch us die.

None of you will see our spring blue sky
nor the summer-yellow flowers' blooms whose life

    is dead to eyes so glazed with winter's bleak decline—
    those whose pockets carry orders they should defy.

Hold out your hand. Accept what I've planted in your mind.
Heed the part that knows we're all of one tribe:

    the all-of-all who hunger love and cry,
    who plough the ground for seed, not flesh and flies.

What will grow from the breakdown of your life
depends on the seeds you carry when that time arrives.

A Sword in Both Hands

One is misled when one looks at the sails and majesty of tall ships instead of their cargo.
—Dionne Brand

We are a camera photographing itself, America.
We are the majesty of tall ships and we are the cargo, America.
We are the jeweled sword and we are the slain.

We raise the blade and knight the brave in Ukraine, America.
We bless them with crowns and say they look like America, America.
We arm them with garlands of dragon-slaying missiles and javelins
of the finest steel.

We bare our sword arm, America, and intone our money prayers.
We strip the evil enemy of coin and commerce. We are money gods,
America.
All this we do with the right hand, America.

With the left we hold a pocked sword notched with brown bodies,
America.
We place the sword in the hands of bonesaw Kings, who do not look
like America, America,
to slay those who the camera cannot see

because we say, America, those brown and far away are not America.
Those who have before them other gods than America are not
America.
Their brave cannot be knighted by our jeweled blades

because only those we say are America, are America, America.
The camera that can only photograph itself, is a mirror
that only sees itself, is a sword that only slays itself,
America.

The Half-Life of Portraits of War

...we survived and were able to bear witness to what happened... To see
that family, the mother and her two children lying there on the ground
lifeless with their little suitcases is the most heartbreaking thing I've seen.
—Lynsey Addario, photojournalist

The witness displayed
her portrait of woe.

I bit my lip, my face wrenched tight.
My rage unmasked, I kicked the cat.

The cat, a victim of war,
does not know

about the towhead child
in the pink puffy coat,

about her big brother in blue,
his little backpack askew.

The cat cowers as I walk by
but soon he forgets and nuzzles

his blunt nose on my leg.
How soon will I forget

the towhead child
her bloodied mother

the brother and friend,
his roller suitcase, the dead?

The witness will not forget.
The soldier who tried to protect

will not forget.

The shooter will not forget.

Only the cat and Putin and
I will forget.

Bodies Responding to Contingent Times

My jaw still aches:
a victim of war.
My tooth and root throb
from incessant grinding

which will pass I am told—although
over there the bodies pile up,
the score will be kept,
the dead will fill the ledgers of woe.

The dentist tells me my teeth are fine.
X-rays reveal no rot or ruined crowns.
She suggests I meditate and wear a mouth guard
to seek relief. I think to tell her about

the dreams that wake me, the tangled sheets,
my visions of hellscapes here after a great undoing.
But I refrain when I see her calming green eyes
fall to her own trembling hands.

To My Wife 42 Years After the Premature Birth of our First Born

The Eternal Female groan'd; it was heard over all the earth.
—William Blake

That time you *aum-ed* away contractions for eight days
after your waters broke too soon.

That time when we convinced the maternity nurse to stop offering you
a little something to take the edge off it, honey.

That time I was afraid of your pain and you showed me:
This is where I grow the world.

That time I held your face and breathed with you, *ha-ha-hoooo*
in time with your heartbeat.

That time you howled the universe into being.

That time when your breast brushed the lips of our preemie.

That time the NICU nurses fell silent in your presence.

That time when you and I and the baby's big brother stripped to skin,
warmed that wired-up boy every day and night until he could sing.

That time no bombs fell.
That time we were not buried in rubble.

That time before this time.

―――――――

Every poem is a translation of silence.
—Manuel Iris

Silent protests and empty placards have become symbols of resistance.
—*The Week,* referring to protests in Russia

I step to the open mic and recite
the empty space between the words. The crowd quiets
and quiets as I quietly hum

    nothing.

A violinist chins her instrument, wafts her hand bowless
over the strings which sing silent to growing things—
to grasses and grain and smoke, all a cacophony of

    hope.

A novelist opens her leafless book and reads
the fourth word down on the sixth absent page, breathes in
and in and in until she sinks to her knees

    replete.

The audience rises to its feet, all applaud one handed,
remove their shoes and pad hushed to the library where each
recites every word from every book missing from every

    empty shelf.

Overhead, a lightening bolt produces no thunder.
A derecho wind does not howl. Here the woman who holds
the blank sign translates the

    silence

into the flux between every heartbeat, the space between
each smudge of ink, every last breath of the dead, every empty
prison cell, each poem not written, every spin of every atom of

———————

The Hospital is a Life is Light is Dust

If I could eat one Cyrillic scripted word,
it would be бомбить*

which means "bomb," from the Greek *bombos*
—a deep and hollow sound,

a sound like sulfur tastes
a burning blue fire on the tongue,

a sound that crumbles a hospital wall.
A woman there births blood and ash.

A child not yet born waits for his mother, waits
for her labor pains, waits…and waits…and waits.

The hospital is everything. Everything is here, waiting,
to be seen if only the light is shined on it.

It is swaddling clothes and it is broken bones.
It is dust and flesh and shattered ears, squalling infants and the
     ready breasts

of a living mother pressed to a dead one's newborn lips.
All the infant wants is mother's milk and mother's flesh and
     mother's eyes.

All the mother wants is her own baby
not to be dust.

All I want is to never have heard this
one deep and hollow sound.

* бомбить, Russian for "bomb," is pronounced: *bəm´ beet*

A Long Rest Interrupted

The gravedigger...starts his days surveying the grounds for new
artillery shells.
                                        —*Washington Post*

The enemy bombs did not disturb our ancient dead.
They had already left their graves—

gone to join the resistance,
gone to stand with their brothers and sisters

at the barricades and bedsides of war.

We will wait to count our fallen.
Now we recite Matins to the living

and number those enemy warriors
we return to their mothers.

At dusk we pray for the day we can
turn battle tanks into tractors,

see our slain become soil for sunflowers,
and our ancient dead return to their rest.

Among Those Who Lay Claim to Ancient Lands

*The border says stop to the wind but the wind speaks another language
and keeps going.*
—Alberto Rios

I stand in a field of stubbled wheat which was
once forest, once sea, once the stuff of stars.
I hold in my hand a tattered deed of a place
some call mine, some call America.

It is a litany of liens, words like carving knives:
grant & bargain, sell & convey,
and—*thence from the stone by the old oak,*
proceed 50 rods to the poplar stump,
these being metes and bounds.

Today, the oak is gone. The stone is buried.

Scrub water maples and locusts struggle
to stand in bad ground used up
by men who held this same deed,
who claimed these same ancient lands.

The deer crash through my fences,
mice chew through my seed bags,
the whistlepigs bulldoze my barn.
None have read the deed.

The tornado, the ice, the deluge all would
wipe this place clean of me, scream *How dare you.*
How dare you possess a place as old as dust.
How dare you carve lines on the living.

I walk, head down, into my house
which weighs heavy on its feet of concrete.

An Open Letter to the Poets, Editors, and Redditors Who Have Moved on from War

Your pages and verse have gone on to chronicle spring.
They note the daffodils that didn't ruin in the hard freeze,
the magnolia blossoms that did, the gander defending the goose,

the news crews which press the President to make war
more interesting, the red carpet preening that floods Reddit threads.
And what's all the rage? The slapped face, billionaires in space—

all while soldiers die and body counts rise. Meanwhile,
the creek is out of its banks, the bottom field submerged,
and the rising waters threaten to sweep away the geese.

So here's your prompt for next week's poem: war
never ends. The dead speak in blank verse.
The dispossessed scatter like bitter alyssum seed.

Witness, The Warring Lords, and the Forever Price

For we are about to destroy this place; because the outcry against them
before the Lord has become so great that the Lord has sent us to destroy it.
—Genesis 19:13

In the beginning it was Lot and
his daughters, his unnamed wife,
and those damnedable angels.

Sodom, Gomorrah, Bucha, Irpin—
all the same: slaughter, panic,
outrage, shame.

This is the stuff of endless lists: the kind and number
of disjointed bones, the chroma tone of burning flesh,
the breadth and width of skin as measured in pain,

kids' skinned knees not kissed, scabs unpicked,
toys crushed, the un-named babies who will never
go to war, the named ones who will.

I rip that page from my embattled Bible.
Overhead, a lone goose sounds like two,
call and response, call and response, so alone.

I look back to the remains of the Terrible Book—
there, the limitless victims and the nameless
wife who I will call *Selah*—

her life as witness as she considers:
her immolate sisters, the lone goose, the good,
the vagrant, the lascivious and chaste.

Her gaze stays fixed
on the crime, forever tied
to the chasmed sky. She sees

the hands that reach from
the graves, the broken crutches,
how blue the fire burns,

how blackened the flesh,
the dirt beneath the fingernails
of the dead, the sins that are not

sins, the sins that are, the gods who
worship their own idols, the idols
made in the image of their savage gods.

Only *Selah* looks back. She knows
the price. She chooses to be
a pillar of salt.

What Passes for Hope in the Time of Apocalypse

The tardigrades
and cockroaches
have no opinion
whether I should
take my iodine tabs
before or after
the missiles
crease the sky.

The Search for War and Peace

It's Palm Sunday and the Pope of Rome calls for peace.
The April air smells like potentiality—like new-mown grass,
like just dug soil, like fresh gunpowder.

Our kitty stalks prey in the front yard, catches a rabbit.
Yesterday it was a snake and I think this is a metaphor
because in Bible stories snakes are more sinister than bunnies.

This same Bible says Jesus rode into Jerusalem on a donkey,
triumphant. But I suspect the creature was confounded by the tangle
of palm fronds and ragged coats laid at his feet.

He did not care that the rabble acclaimed his rider as King,
just that the stench and shouts of the crowd were too much,
that he craved the craziness to cease, yearned to graze, to be relieved

of his burden—which may be a metaphor too because his burden
was the Prince of Peace. The Pope did not pray for the donkey.
Neither did he pray for the bunny or cat—

though peace between cat and rabbit would be a good thing.
Don't raid our garden for carrots and peas, dear Leporidae,
you, the queen of breeding. And you, Cat. Stop being a cat.
     Just stop.

This is the message of the Pope of Rome who does not mention
that declawed cats are more likely to bite, that the venom
of snakes can raise the dead, that rabbit meat

was prized by monks during lent, that the word for peace
in Ukrainian is *mir,* that the word for peace in Russian is *mir,*
that Google searches for "war" are five times that of
     searches for "peace."

The Last Line Spoken by the Actor Playing Lear

...that everything will end with a nuclear strike... is more probable than the other outcome... But we will go to heaven, while [you] will simply croak.

—Vladimir Solovyov, Russian State TV

The actor playing Lear looks to the balcony
as if seeking there an answer to a question
he can't quite remember. He thinks
of the groceries he's to pick up,
—the audience sits silent—
next, to himself, he asks *to be or not to be?*
but that isn't it,
—the audience still silent—
he gathers himself in the quiet,
takes a breath, sighs into his cupped hands
—the audience rustles—
he begins, *O, reason not the need!*
forgets, skips ahead, *Man's life*
is cheap as beasts. He stops again,
he knows something we don't. Backstage
he's read: the missiles fly, there is no
hope. The show must go on. He rips
his kingly robe, says the line again,
Man's life is cheap as beasts and again
Man's life is cheap as beasts and again
Man's life...

In the Days Before I Die, I Recall the Last Time I Was Here
—for Vanda Semyonovna Obiedkova

The tongue of huddling in cellars is a forgotten one, a language
only a few of us remember from the before times. But here I am,
again, buried in this frigid basement beneath these same shamed streets.

I should be home, folding laundry, making *khrustykys* for the little ones,
maybe napping. Instead, I shiver away the last of what was me
covered only by my daughter's thin coat.

> I recall my father, gone to dust in the gulag days, his sure hand
> firm over my small mouth, held my crying inside as Nazis hunted
> for my kind in the homes above our blacked-out hiding place.

I beg for water but it's really the dark that defeats me, steals these
last shallow breaths of mine. I dream back to that time when
10-year-old me first learned the lightless dialect of cellar life,

was forever drained of light. Since then, it has been the daily
illuminated hours that have saved me—that made the thin link
from one frightful night to the next—and without that dim lit bridge

> I am already dead.

Dreams of a Recent Refugee Alone and a Long Way From Home

How can I leave my little nest?
—Lidia Constantinopla Havrilenko
83-year-old Ukrainian refugee

The rocket bombs
left my village
rubbled with bodies
buried beneath hearth stones,
tore door jam spiders from their webs.
Jackdaw carcasses litter
the barren ground.
I carry two small sacks
—sweet Keecha Cat in one,
my wedding veil and a faded
photo of my dear Taras
in the other—us crammed
onto a train headed to a place,
of strangers. I ride west
in the shadow of vultures' wings,
resigned that the light shining
on their blue-black feathers
is robbed from me. I recall
my town, Bakhmut, in shades
of gray except for what wafted
from the bakery, the aroma
of fresh-baked rye
sapphire in my mind,
like the sky into which
the waving grain grew, the same
blue from which the missiles flew.
I hear again the silence
before they struck,
remember the sleep not slept
since before the war when night
was star dark, not lit by

hunger, not tinged broken
and dust-white and frightened
by its own blindness. And here
so far from there, all I want to do
is go back home, to my little nest,
even if it is to sit amidst
the debris, on the remains
of the tattered sofa where
I suckled my son, now
a broken man, to fill him
again with the milk
of our tribe's mettle
so he can drive the vermin
from our lands and we,
like the spiders, can
reweave our webs,
like jackdaws, re-feather our nests,
like humans begin to plan
our revenge. But maybe
not this time. I just
want to die quiet
in my little nest
with my little
Keecha Cat
and the photo
of my dear Taras
hung back
on its wall.

Mariupol, Mỹ Lai, Dresden, Tigray

—A found poem from Kurt Vonnegut's *Slaughterhouse-Five*

All of this happened /   more or less /
and even if / the wars / keep coming
like glaciers / there would still / be
Plain Old Death.
/ My God /
   /what have
they done ? This. This. This is /
   this is a broken kite /
in the imagination of combat's fans /
/ the divine-
ly listless / love / play / that follows the orgasm
of victory / it is called /
 mopping up. / All time
/ is all time.
It / does not change.
/ It / does not
lend it / self to warnings. It simply is.
 We will
all live
forever, no matter how
  / dead
we may sometimes seem to be / life /
/ is /
  / so short. And jumbled /
 / and jangled /
there is
nothing
    intelligent to say
about a massacre / Everybody
is supposed to be dead / to never say
anything
to never want / anything /
ever
again. Everything is supposed to be /

very quiet and it always is / except for the birds /
/ and what
do the birds say? / All / there is to say /
 about a massacre /
things like "Poo-tee-weet?"
I am not overjoyed. / Everything is /
all right, and everybody / has to do
exactly what he does / / / / / So it goes.
Again. Again. Again.

Demi-Sonnet for the Dead

I am pro plain-pine-box, pro urn of ash,
pro mortality and dust and bodies
decaying into dirt—except when
bulldozed into ditches. I am *not* pro ditches,
not pro pits dug by victims, not pro pleading
or pushing into crypts. The burying of bodies
should be done by hand, one sifted fistful at a time,
dirt mixed with tears. Sometimes blood.

The Kind of Silence Heard When Musicians are Murdered

—For Yuri Kerpatenko, murdered by Russian authorities for refusing to conduct a concert in occupied Kherson

What if the whole idea is wrong?
What if music played at the point of a gun

could resurrect the dead? What if there really are
ten dimensions of space and time?

What if one of those dimensions
were notes on a symphony's score

that, one by one, disappeared
but only when played perfectly?

A cantata could become silence

the more it is performed—the conductor's baton
sweeping arcs, outlining the shape of empty space

so the music can rise into it—like a swarm
of bees, like a murmuration of note-shaped starlings.

And what if the violinists bowed on infinite strings
—thrummed light into the night sky

while at the same time the kettledrum's mallets struck
the stretched skin of

the one creature not named by Adam?

And what if the conductor himself, bound
at the wrists by a burning rope, is dragged

off by the authorities for playing so perfectly—
so perfectly that the disbelievers, the tyrants,

the martial marchers—all strut
to the rhythm of their own oblivion?

And what if the strutters can never know the kind of quiet
that depends on autumn leaves falling,

the quiet that breaks hearts, the quiet
that is more dangerous than nothing—

the silence that's heard by every one

of us who's sat quiet among friends,
mourned the ones murdered

for beauty—who we'd welcome
to fill their bellies with fire,

then sing courage-hymns to the poets
and painters, hope to the story-tellers,

even as one of their own lies sprawled
on the floor at his home in a surprising pool
        of blood?

The War Crimes of Ordinary Men

As soon as thought tries to engage itself with evil...it is frustrated because it finds nothing there. That is the banality of evil.
—Hannah Arendt

I hike in the prairie at the far reach of the farm. I hear
from an adjoining field the clack of a dozer, a racket that drowns
out the bunting and bobolink chitter nearby.
Under the earthmover's tread

threads of mycelium tangled and talking with the grasses,
voles in their burrows, ants tunneling
sand from the deep places—all crushed. The birds
above continue their chorus, keep seeking mates

rustling the grasses—until they and I both start
at a rifle's crack and the blasts of pop bottles shattered
with copper-clads. Rabbits and I scatter into the woods.
The chirp and trill in the trees ceases, sudden as the shot.

I sit with my back to a trunk, shelter in the shade, a place
safe from my fears. The chitter resumes, my breathing settles
as I remember—this is not a place at war. The yahoos mean
no harm. They are not the kind who would decide after a "howdy,"

a good enough smile, and us walking from each other,
to turn, shoulder their rifles and drop me
with a shot in the back. They are not the kind
to pick the seed from my pocket, the ring off my finger.

As the birds continue their chorus,
these ordinary men would never
watch blankly as blood seeped from me
into the loamy spring ground.

To the Person Wondering Why We Are Called Wanderers

An apartment building in Odesa.
A missile attack. A woman survives.

Let's call her Hanelle. You'll note
she looks a lot like me.

She packs her few bags in a cart and sets off,
carried by a stream of refugees

from pogrom & blight, famine & war
and joins the old ones unwinding their lives

back to Vilnius this time, or Cologne or Krakau—
where she opens a little shop, sells pins and needles

to folks like you who say she is a good Jew,
can be trusted, but not with the kids, right?

Never with your kids because you'd heard the rumors
of the blooding and though such tales could not be true

about Hanelle, you can never tell. And when the mob
comes and proclaims that it had been proved

it was the Jews who brought this latest plague,
you pick up a torch, too, are among the first

to kindle the flame which Hanelle barely escapes
with her baby on her back, a sack

of pins and needles, her silver shabbat candle sticks,
and her great great grandmother's mezuzah.

She rides in the cart on her way again
to Kyiv, to Odesa, to Uman, to Kharkiv.

Eating Pistachios Over Morning Coffee While Talking About War and Other Things

The pile of pistachio shells grows
more on Deb's plate than mine. Both of us split
and eat, split and eat—take turns talking
about the tender feelings of an offended friend, nursing
little hurts, tear up about how we've stopped caring

so much for the war in Ukraine. And that's the thing,
the suffering continues. Bloodied bodies pile up. Folks
throw hulking chess pieces at each other, the queens
and kings command the pawns to drop bigger bombs
into each teams' zigzag trenches.

Just so you know, I am not both-sidesing. Yes, there is
an invader and an invaded—but I cannot help thinking
that bigger bombs may not be better even as I cheer the delivery
of Switchblades® and Stingers® and Rugers® and rockets
to the good guys—and profits to Raytheon.

I guess I am bullish on defense stocks. I ignore the irony
of them being called "defense stocks." I sweep spent
pistachio shells into the palm of one hand while the other
pokes at my phone for drone shots of blown-up Russian tanks.
I hope I won't see body parts because Russian body parts

were once parts of people. But I do see them, the nearby fields
salted with hunks of mothers' sons and it's all too much. I start
my morning chores, take the refuse from breakfast
to the compost pile, check to see if my Havahart®
has protected our ripening strawberries from the chipmunks.

It hasn't. The plot is a mess, strewn with wounded fruit
so I go back inside, get on-line and order a pack of snap traps,
upping the arms race between me and the rodents.

The Hungry Times and Uncertain Skies

In Izium, autumn brings days of light rain
and cool nights, the hornbeam leaves begin
to yellow,

and Russian man-boys abandon
their idling tanks and still-warm MREs.
They've left behind horror pits where flesh drapes

off chains. In their wake are tangled graves
beneath the trees—and abettors who betray
neighbors in exchange for grain.

But now there's victory on the news wires. The headline
writers tease a tale of bad times gone good, of
locals freed by casualty-free masters of the battle map.

The clockworks of war have seemingly sprung—
undone from ordinary time. The hour hand runs
back to when the dead were not

dead. The minute hand gyres forward—
towards the days when the invader's flags are cut down,
the Blue and Yellow is raised by war-worn hands.

Though, to those who have remained in this ravaged town,
it's the second hand—a syringe, savage and thin—
that twitches back and forth marking

no time. It is a quivering fear that, in the absence
of the enemy, retreats and takes up
defensive positions inside each survivor's head.

The fright looks out through dilate eyes, shifting,
still primed for menace and threat. The people
are stuck between

the terrored past and a dubious future. All
are split in two—both halved and whole, parts
tethered together by a slack-line of time—

one part free, one captive. All they've eaten
is weeds, moldered melons, apples
blighted on the trees, and wormy grain.

The relief of liberation is too much to digest
on their near-empty stomachs. These folks are free
to spend no money

in stores with empty shelves. They know
Russians hide, neighbors seem too fattened,
and the sky might at any moment turn to fire.

The Choices Men Make

I see a man in a passing truck, red F-150, Ohio plates. He tosses
a Mickey D's slushie-cup out his window.

It splats in the ditch, a blue, ice-chip grenade, scatters
lid and straw and sharded plastic among the grasses.

This feels personal.

Missiles are like this. Follow the fire back to the launching point,
and there you will find a man

who aims the thing, another who pulls the firing pin—towards
a train station, a maternity hospital, a nuclear power plant.

The moments after detonation are not the ones to ask the rabbi:
How long should we sit shiva

for the demise of a reactor vessel? How long should we
wear black

for all the buried brides in white, the grooms in rented blue suits
and their children—ulcered raw and burned?

How long will the land be unsettled with a specter
that will only produce tumored women and mutant making men?

The soil of nations will grow decrepit and alone—
empty of humans, dismal as their tombs.

Ghazal For the Trees

In the forest nothing is ever mute.
—from "The Forest Song,"
by Leslya Ukrainka, poet, activist

The great oaks of Ukraine will soon wear their autumn-brown leaves.
From Kharkiv to Odesa there will be whispering among the trees.

The birches will be naked soon, their branches scissor-cut against the sky—
as they were before the war when nothing had yet undone the trees.

Near Lviv, the pines confer about what they've heard from the front.
Underground their roots are the speaking tongues of the trees.

Before the days of the Cossacks who swept in from the steppes, before
Ukrainian was spoken, the ancient Maksym Oak was king of the trees.

It cast its shadow on the thousand battles that raged at its feet,
limbs stretched skyward, away from the blood and bodies that fed the trees.

In the east, the enemy flees, leaves tortured corpses, hunger, disease.
The oaks shudder in the sullen air that's clung to the trees.

Is this what it's like before the flash of the atom, before the breach
and mushroom-cloud seething that shatters the trunks of trees?

Or is this a hint of peace, when *babusyas* emerge from cellars to embrace
their warrior-kin who left before summer sprung green in the trees?

The slight sounds of winter: the shush of falling snow on the beeches,
the rustle of the remaining leaves, sleet ticking on what's clung to the trees.

I've no more poems about this war, its tattered flags and buried bones. Its grief.
Now, again, is the time for *The Forest Song* to be sung to the trees.

Notes on Selected Poems

Holodomor:
The "Terror Famine" inflicted on Ukrainians by Soviet Russia in the early 1930s.

Among Those Who Lay Claim to Ancient Lands:
Putin's claim to Ukrainian land is doubly absurd when I consider how we people can lay claim to land at all.

What Passes for Hope in the Time of Apocalypse:
There is no sane response to nuclear apocalypse. To pretend there is—or that a person can control his or her circumstances in the face of such calamity—is madness. And yet, my first response to Putin's "waving the nuclear sword" was to check the availability of potassium iodide on Amazon.

Witness, The Warring Lords and the Forever Price:
After the photo of Volodymyr Zelensky Bearing witness to the horrors inflicted on Bucha.

In the Days Before I Die, I Recall the Last Time I Was Here:
For Vanda Semyonovna Obiedkova who, in 1941 Mariupol, hid in a basement from the Nazis and in 2022 died hiding from the Russians in a basement in Mariupol.

Mariupol, Mỹ Lai, Dresden, Tigray:
To quote Kurt Vonnegut's *Slaughter House Five,* "All of this happened."

The War Crimes of Ordinary Men:
The footage is chilling in its banality. Soldiers casually shoot two unarmed civilians in the back, rummage through their pockets and then, just as casually, scavenge the dead men's property. They find some alcohol, pour each other drinks and toast. They look just like my neighbors (some of whom are fond of guns and afternoons of target practice)—ordinary, fun-having and harmless. The soldiers' actions, as evil as they are, seem positively banal.

Ghazal For the Trees:

Lesya Ukrainka, was a 19th century giant of Ukrainian national identity and letters who wrote the epic fantasy/poem/play "The Forest Song."

Dick Westheimer has—in the company of his wife and writing companion Debbie—lived, gardened and raised five children on their plot of land in rural southwest Ohio. Dick has enjoyed picking bluegrass music with his neighbors and running and walking the trails on his and nearby farms. He is a *Rattle* Poetry Prize finalist and his most recent poems have appeared in *Whale Road Review, Minyan, Rattle, Paterson Review, Chautauqua Review, Gyroscope Review, Northern Appalachia Review, Anti-Heroin Chic, Sheila-Na-Gig online, Pine Mountain Sand and Gravel*, and *Cutthroat*. More at dickwestheimer.com

Sheila-Na-Gig Editions

www.ingramcontent.com/pod-product-compliance
Lightning Source LLC
Chambersburg PA
CBHW030526130626
46549CB00007B/3122